NOODLE COOKBOOK

THE BEST NOODLE RECIPES FROM THAILAND AND BEYOND

SARAH MILLER

CONTENTS

Introduction   v

1. Noodle Recipes   1
2. High and Dry Recipes   16
3. Desserts   60

Conclusion   65

INTRODUCTION

Asian cuisine is found in every nook and cranny of the world. Be it as street food or even in the classiest restaurants, Asian cuisine never fails to delight us. The richness of flavor, the beautiful aromas wafting up to our noses, makes our mouths water. How many times have we wished that we could recreate these same recipes in the comfort of our kitchen? Well, your time has now come! It's time to stop imagining and time to start cooking! It's your time to shine and impress everyone around you with your prowess in cooking and specialize in Asian cuisine.

Discover a whole new world of noodles; there are just so many different types that you can never have enough of them. This cookbook focuses mainly on a collection of several noodle dishes inspired from all over these countries. You've got yourself a collection of 30 delicious easy to make recipes.

So, put on that chef's hat, that you've always wanted and cooked your way through this maze of flavors and aromas. It's time to cook that delectable feast you always wanted. Be it the traditional Pho, Filipino Pancit or even the two surprise desserts, in the end, this cookbook will cater to every need and taste and leave everyone around you in absolute awe of your cooking abilities.

1

NOODLE RECIPES

Lemongrass - Tofu Soupy Noodles

Want an extra burst of happiness or some energy to brighten your day? This dish is the solution. Creamy, nutritious, and comforting, this noodle soup is very easy to cook and convenient, making it a popular delicacy. A wonderful combination of vegetable broth and coconut milk, this dish is a perfect, wholesome meal to have at any time of the day. Savor the aroma of lemongrass to feel the peace and sanctity. A flavor you will never forget, this dish is fulfilling for both the mind and body.

Ingredients:

- 10 ounces of noodles
- 4-6 cups vegetable broth
- 1-2 stalks minced lemongrass
- ½ packet medium/soft tofu, cubed
- 3 inches ginger
- 1 broccoli head
- 2 sliced cabbages
- 2 Chinese cabbages, chopped
- 4 tbsp soy sauce
- ½ cup of coconut milk
- Chilis/chili sauce
- ¼ cup chopped basil

Preparation Time: 30 minutes
Serving Size: 2
Instructions:

1. Boil water in another utensil. Add the rice noodles and cook them. Once properly cooked, drain them under cold water. To avoid sticking of the noodles, you may immediately divide them into serving bowls or toss them with a little bit of oil.

2. Take a soup pot. Add the stock, lemongrass, ginger, lemon juice and carrots. Boil the contents and add remaining vegetables. Reduce the heat and cook until the vegetables soften.

3. Minimize the heat and add coconut milk and tofu. Stir gently to keep the tofu from falling apart.

4. Taste the soup and add soy sauce, chili sauce or chilies, and lime juice according to your preference.

5. Add this soup to the serving bowls containing the noodles.

6. Top with fresh basil and serve piping hot.

Singaporean Veggie Delight

Noodle soups are the epitome of comfort food, and this recipe is no exception. Full of flavor and aroma, the soup contains a blend of all healthy veggies combined with a bit of spice to give a smooth, creamy soup. A perfect companion for a low day, this dish is brimming with nutrients and very easy to make.

Ingredients:

- ½ cup of rice noodles
- 1 chopped onion
- 15-20 beans
- 1 chopped carrot
- 1 cup cauliflower

- 1 cup cabbage
- 2 cloves of garlic
- 2 tsp chili sauce
- 2 tsp soya sauce
- Salt

Preparation Time - 20 minutes

Serving Time - 2

Instructions:

1. Add all the vegetables to a pressure cooker. Pour water and cook until soft. Let the veggies cool completely

2. Take out 1-2 tbsp of the cooked vegetables. Add the remaining vegetables to a blender and grind to a thin paste.

3. Boil water in another utensil. Add the rice noodles and cook them. Once properly cooked, drain them under cold water.

4. Add the sauces and the paste with sauce to taste. Boil the mixture for a few minutes. Do not overcook the noodles.

5. Take off the heat and serve hot with pepper powder.

ComPHO food

Pho ("fuh"), an aromatic dish filled with the goodness of

crisp fresh veggies, tender, juicy meat, and a mouthwatering broth is a traditional Vietnamese soup and the epitome of comfort food. True pho is made from beef bones, but you can use chicken broth instead. A rough day, unbearable work pressure, a beautiful rainy afternoon, a lazy weekend, for every mood every day, the Vietnamese aromas will be a promising highlight to the day and give the much-needed comfort.

Ingredients:

For the broth:

- 6 cups of chicken broth
- 2 whole star anise
- 2 onions - large
- 3 carrots, peeled and coarsely chopped
- 1 piece of ginger (4")
- 3 whole cloves
- 2 cinnamon sticks (3")
- 2 teaspoons of coriander seeds
- 3 teaspoons of fish sauce
- 3 teaspoons of tamari or soy sauce

For Serving:

- 1 cup of chicken breast - thinly sliced
- 1 cup of dried rice noodles (banh pho)
- 3 medium-sized scallions
- 8 ounces mung bean sprouts
- 8 ounces fresh herbs of your choice
- 1 fresh chili pepper

- 2 lemons
- Hot sauce or Sriracha sauce

Preparation Time - 60 min
Serving Size - 4
Instructions:

1. Peel the ginger and onions then cut them into quarters.

2. Char the ginger and onions thoroughly all over on the gas stove with the use of tongs, until they are partly charred. Remove any loose excessively charred parts by running them through cold water.

3. Place the star cloves, anise, cinnamon, and coriander seeds in a pan and roast over medium-low heat until toasted and very fragrant. Ensure the spices are not burnt by constantly stirring them.

4. Take another saucepan and add the chicken broth, fish sauce, soy sauce, carrots, and charred vegetables.

5. Boil the broth over medium-high heat. Once it boils, reduce the flame to medium-low and let it simmer for about 30 minutes to let all the spices and aromas infuse into the broth.

6. Boil water in another utensil. Add the rice noodles and cook them. Once properly cooked, drain them under cold water. To avoid sticking of the noodles, you may immediately divide them into serving bowls or toss them with a little bit of oil.

7. Thinly slice the chili pepper and the scallions. Cut the lime into thin wedges. Arrange them along with mung beans in a serving dish. The herbs are to be roughly chopped. This serves as the rest of the pho toppings.

8. Once the broth is ready, strain it and discard the solids. Heat the broth over low heat. There should be ample amounts of steam, but do not let the broth boil.

9. Divide the noodles into serving bowls and add the raw chicken slices on top. Spread them evenly to ensure that the broth can cook the slices thoroughly.

10. Pour the broth evenly in each bowl over the meat slices. The broth will start to cook them immediately and they will turn opaque.

11. Serve the pho at the table and let people use toppings as they wish.

Easy Peasy Ramen

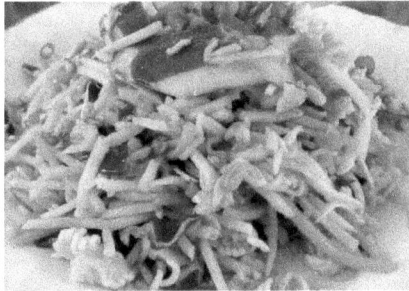

Ramen noodles are extremely popular throughout the world and pretty much classifies as a form of comfort food. A perfect combination of veggies and protein, it's a wholesome meal for any occasion. This yummy and healthy easy-to-make homemade recipe will definitely fill your hungry tummy. The hard boil egg slices just add to the beauty of this dish and also add on some extra protein.

Ingredients:

- 8 ounces ramen noodles
- 1 tablespoon olive oil
- 2 eggs
- 1 tablespoon ginger, freshly grated
- 4 cloves minced garlic
- 4 cups of chicken broth
- 1 tablespoon of soy sauce
- 4 ounces of shiitake mushrooms
- 2 tablespoons of chopped chives
- 1 carrot, grated
- 3 cups baby spinach

Preparation Time - 30 min

Serving Time - 4

Instructions:

1. Hard boil the eggs. Peel them and cut into halves.

2. In a large pot, heat the oil and add ginger, garlic and stir for a few minutes until fragrant.

3. Add the chicken broth, soy sauce, mushrooms and 3 cups of water and stir. Add the noodles.

4. Boil the contents, reduce the heat and simmer until the mushrooms have softened.

5. Add the spinach, carrots, and chives and cook till the spinach leaves wilt.

6. Garnish it with eggs and serve immediately.

The Malaysian Laksa

Laksa is a traditional Malaysian dish, popular for the Laksa paste, a blend of the choicest spices ground thoroughly giving rise to a strong, spicy flavor. The rich, creamy broth made from coconut milk is mixed with tender meat or seafood and Laksa Paste. This promising, easy to make dish is a wonderful opportunity to explore the exotic world of Asian spices.

Ingredients:

- 24 ounces chicken breast cubed
- 16 ounces peeled raw shrimp (large)
- 16 ounces of rice noodles
- 6 cups of chicken broth
- 3 tbsp of vegetable oil
- 8 lime leaves
- 1 tbsp brown sugar
- 1 tsp salt
- 5 cups of coconut milk
- Juice from 1-2 lemons
- 1 tbsp fish sauce

Homemade Laksa Paste:

- 3-5 dried chilies
- 3-5 shallots, chopped
- 2 tbsp dried shrimp
- 4 garlic cloves
- ½ cup chopped lemongrass
- 3 tbsp ginger finely chopped
- 12 soaked cashews
- 2 tsp turmeric powder
- 2 tsp coriander, ground
- 1 tsp cumin, ground
- 1 tsp paprika, sweet
- 3 tbsp peanut oil

Preparation Time - 1 hour
Serving Time - 8
Instructions:
Laksa Paste:

1. Keep the dried shrimp and chilies for 20 min in a small bowl of boiling water. Add all the ingredients except for the oil in a food processor. Drain the shrimps and chili and add them as well. Blend well into a fine paste.

2. Add oil and blend to a fine paste.

Laksa Broth and Noodles:

1. Boil water in another utensil. Add the rice noodles and cook them. Once properly cooked, drain them under cold water. To avoid sticking of the noodles, you may immediately divide them into serving bowls or toss them with a little bit of oil.

2. Heat a soup pot over medium heat. Add all the Laksa paste and sauté till the color becomes deeper and more fragrant.

3. Add chicken broth, lime leaves, salt, and sugar and bring down to a simmer.

4. Add the chicken and shrimp and cook for a few minutes. Add coconut milk after 4-5 minutes. Simmer the mixture but do not let it boil.

5. Add lemon juice and fish sauce to taste. There should be a rich, slightly salty taste.

6. Ladle the soup over the pre-divided noodles in the serving bowl. Garnish with bean sprouts and cilantro.

7. Serve with lime wedges and chili sauce.

Crystal Clear

This chicken noodle soup recipe is the epitome of soul food. The fresh crunch of the vegetable gives the juicy tender meat some wonderful company and will definitely bring a smile to your face. A simple and easy-to-make dish, the warmth of the broth coupled with a light flavor of spices will certainly lift your spirits any day.

Ingredients:

- 8 ounces of rice noodles
- 10 ounces of chicken
- ½ inch ginger, grated
- 1 crushed garlic clove
- Few bunches of cai xin
- Fried shallots
- Sliced chili

Preparation Time - 25 minutes

Serving Size - 4

Instructions:

1. Boil a pot of water and take off the flame. Soak noodles in them until cooked. Drain, cool and set aside

2. Add ginger, garlic and chicken stock in a large pan. Simmer on medium heat.

3. Add the chicken and bring the heat down to low. Simmer until the chicken is completely cooked.

4. Take the chicken out of the stock and shred.

5. Add cai xin to the soup and boil for a minute.

6. Stir the drained noodles and shredded chicken in the broth.

7. Divide the contents between 4 bowls and serve with shallots and sliced chili.

8. Your bowl of comfort is now ready to eat!

Classic Mohinga

Mohinga is a Burmese treasure chest of vibrant colors and flavors. This dish contains freshly ground, roasted jasmine rice flour giving the soup its creamy texture and richness. Each ingredient plays its own crucial role, the high-light being the aroma of lemongrass which counteracts the fishy taste of the soup. This rich dish is a must-have on any special family occasion. Easily a favorite, it will leave you and your family wanting more.

Ingredients:

- ½ cup uncooked jasmine rice
- Broth:
- 12 cups water
- 2 teaspoons salt
- 48 ounces of catfish meat
- 2 ounces ginger cut into slabs
- 5 bay leaves
- ½ tsp white pepper, ground
- ½ tbsp black pepper, ground

Soup:

- 10 ounces of rice noodles
- ¼ cup garlic, minced
- 3 tbsp minced ginger
- 1 minced stalk of lemongrass
- I tsp turmeric
- I tbsp paprika powder
- 2 diced red onions
- Salt
- ¼ cup of fish sauce
- ⅓ cup vegetable oil

Serving:

- ½ cup chopped cilantro
- 2 lemons, cut into wedges
- Thinly sliced red onions
- 6 slice hard-boiled eggs

Preparation Time - 1 hour 40 min
Serving Size - 6
Instructions:
Mohinga:

1. Heat an oven to 350°F. Take the rimmed baking pan and spread the rice over it. Stir the rice occasionally to give a golden brown color with a beautiful aroma. Cool and thoroughly grind to a thin powder.

2. Take a pot large enough to fit the catfish. Add lemongrass, ginger, water, peppers, bay leaf, and salt. Boil the ingredients. Then, simmer on a lower heat.

3. Lower the fish into the pot. Simmer the contents and then cook gently for 15 minutes.

4. Rotate the fish to ensure full coverage and cook for until flesh comes away from the bone. Take out the fish.

5. Discard the skin off the fish. Separate meat from the skeleton, keeping the skeleton intact. Put the skeleton back in the pot.

6. Boil the contents. Then reduce heat and simmer for 15 minutes. There should be a mild lemongrass flavor with a cloudy appearance.

7. Strain the broth and then return to the pot

8. Mix together some of the broth and the rice powder in a small bowl till the lumps dissolve. Mix this with the broth in the pot. Simmer and stir until it starts to thicken and then reduce the heat. Gently simmer the broth.

9. Take a wok and heat oil over high heat. Add the ginger, lemongrass and stir.

10. Add the cooked fish, paprika, turmeric and mix the fish gently so it turns to a coarse paste.

11. Add this to the broth and simmer. Add onions and fish sauce. Simmer for some more time the flavors mix together.

12. Taste the broth. It should be a bit salty to compensate for the blandness of the noodles.

13. Boil a pot of water and take off the flame. Soak noodles in them until cooked. Drain, cool and set aside

14. Divide the noodles into the serving bowls. Pour the soup over them and serve with egg slices, cilantro, and lemon wedges.

2

HIGH AND DRY RECIPES

Vietnamese Noodle Salad

A light and invigorating vermicelli noodle plate of crisp chopped veggies in a tangy Vietnamese rice vinegar dressing makes it an amazing side dish or an entree. Present it with grilled meats, chicken or tofu in case you are a vegan, best served cold. Avoid the hassle of cooking noodles over a flame with this easy recipe. Enjoy the rejuvenating flavor of this dish and satiate your appetite with some healthy snacking.

Ingredients:

- 12 ounces vermicelli noodles
- ½ cup of seasoned rice vinegar
- ¼ tsp of crushed red pepper
- ⅓ cup chopped cilantro
- 2 shredded carrots
- 4 chopped green onions
- 2 shredded cucumber
- 1 ½ cup bean sprouts
- 3 tbsp sugar
- ½ cup of fish sauce
- 2 minced cloves of garlic
- Lemon

Preparation Time - 30 min
Serving Time - 4
Instructions:

1. Soak vermicelli noodles by soaking them in boiling water until soft.

2. Add the cucumbers, carrots, sprouts, and cilantro to noodles.

3. Mix the rice vinegar, fish sauce, sugar, red pepper, and garlic. Mix well to remove any sugar clumps.

4. Add ¾ of the dressing to the noodles then toss gently. If needed, add in more dressing.

5. Garnish with cilantro and lemon juice.

Thai Nuts n Noodles

Thai Nuts n Noodles is a delicious combination of noodles, vegetables, and a sweet, spicy, and nutty sauce. This quick recipe requires nothing extra and can be made out of the simplest of veggies lying in your pantry. A great dish to have for a weekend dinner date or simply spending some time with family; the authentic Thai sauce is sure to leave you craving for more. Definitely a better substitute for hotel takeout!

Ingredients:

- 16 ounces of ramen
- ¼ cup of vegetable oil
- 1 red bell pepper, finely chopped
- 3 finely chopped cloves of garlic
- 1 finely chopped carrot
- 1 tablespoon honey
- ⅓ cup of soy sauce
- 1 teaspoon chili sauce

- ¼ cup of peanut butter
- ¼ cup of sliced green onions
- ⅓ cup of chopped peanuts
- 1 teaspoon sesame seeds

Preparation Time - 25 minutes

Serving Size - 4

Instructions:

1. Cook the noodles till soft in boiling water and then drain and set aside.

2. Mix the soy sauce, peanut butter, chili sauce, and honey together in a cup.

3. Heat the oil in a large fry pan. Sauté the bell peppers, carrots, and garlic.

4. Add the pasta and sauce into the frying pan. Toss lightly until properly combined.

5. Garnish with chopped peanuts, green onions, sesame seeds, and cilantro.

6. Serve hot!

Holy Basil!

This Thai dish combines the freshness of basil and a beautiful crunch of fresh vegetables and is made over a bed of rice noodles. This is a gluten-free recipe, ideal for all the vegans out there. The sauce is a rich, creamy Thai-style pesto sauce which is then tossed with Thai rice noodles. Include a garnish of ground cashews in addition to a little crisp basil, and you have a noodle dish that will fulfill your most grounded noodle desires. Delightful to serve, these noodles likewise make an extraordinary dish to serve any present company and at social gatherings.

Ingredients:

- 6-10 ounces flat noodles
- 2 tbsp of vegetable oil
- 8-10 leaves of fresh basil
- Finely ground or chopped cashews

For Basil Sauce:

- ½ cup of fresh green basil
- ⅓ cup of roasted and unsalted cashews
- 4 tbsp coconut oil
- 3-4 garlic cloves
- 1 ½ tbsp of soy sauce (wheat-free)
- 1 tbsp lemon juice
- 1 minced red chili

Preparation Time - 20 min
Serving Size - 3

Instructions:

1. Boil water in a large pot. Add salt. Pour the noodles and cook until they soften. Do not overcook them.

2. Add all the ingredients for the basil sauce in a blender. Blend thoroughly to make the sauce.

3. Keep a large frypan over a medium flame and add oil. When you next add the noodles, you will hear a sizzling sound indicating that the pan is hot enough.

4. Toss the noodles gently.

5. Add 2 tbsp of the basil sauce and continue to stir fry until the noodles are soft yet still chewy. If the texture is not as desired, you may add more sauce and continue frying until you get the desired texture.

6. Remove the pan from the heat and add the remaining sauce. Toss gently but properly.

7. Add salt, lime juice, chili, and soy sauce as per your requirements.

8. Garnish with the cashews and fresh basil leaves and enjoy!

Vegan Haven

Pad Thai, a traditional Thai recipe, is popular throughout the world. This recipe is perfect for a light, healthy meal. The nutty garnish will give you a wonderful crunchy feeling. Made out of rice noodles, it is gluten-free, thus popular with vegans and ideal for the health-conscious foodies. The fresh garden collection of this dish brings with it lots of nutrition and flavor and a delicious dish for any kind of party.

Ingredients:

- 8 ounces of pad Thai noodles
- 3 tbsp of diced onion
- 4 minced cloves of garlic
- ½ cup soft tofu
- 3-4 heads of baby bok choy
- 2 sliced spring onions
- 3 cups of bean sprouts
- ¼ cup of crushed roasted peanuts
- ⅓ cup of cilantro
- 4 tbsp oil
- 2-3 tbsp veg stock
- Lemon wedges

For Pad Thai Sauce:

- ¼ cup of vegetable stock
- 3 ½ tbsp soy sauce
- ¾ tbsp tamarind sauce
- ½-1 tsp chili sauce
- 3 tbsp brown sugar

Preparation Time - 25 minutes

Serving Size - 2

Instructions:

1. Boil water in a large pot. Add salt. Pour the noodles and cook until they soften. Do not overcook them.

2. Mix the soy sauce, sugar, tamarind sauce, and vegetable stock. Ensure the sugar completely dissolves. Ensure the sauce has a very strong taste (sour-sweet and then salty-spicy)

3. In a large preheated fry pan, add oil and sauté the minced onion and garlic, till fragrance is released

4. Add the bok choy and enough stock to keep the contents frying. Continue to cook until the bok choy is green and soft.

5. You may add more oil if the contents appear to be dry.

6. Add the noodles and ⅓ the sauce. Toss gently.

7. Continue heating the noodles on medium-high flame.

8. Keep adding the sauce and stir fry till noodles are soft, chewy and sticky and till all the sauce is poured in the noodles.

9. Add the soft tofu along with the final part of the sauce. Stir nicely to mix the tofu in with the contents.

10. Take off the heat and add the bean sprouts, spring onion and ¾ of nuts.

11. Toss gently and add more soy sauce if you want more flavor.

12. Serve hot with lemon wedges on the side.

The Herbiary

Attempt this simple Thai noodle formula made with crisp herbs. It's snappy and easy to make, and super-delicious! Great both for veggie lovers, or you may simply include shrimp or chicken some extra protein. The herbs exude a tantalizing aroma, which leaves your mouth watering. Perfect for any meal of the day, this dish is a must-have to add to your healthy meal plans.

Ingredients:

- 8 ounces of noodles
- ¼ cup of crushed dry peanuts
- 1 cup medium-firm tofu (cubed)
- 2-3 tbsp vegetable broth
- For the Spice Paste:
- 3 minced cloves of garlic
- 1 red/green chili
- 3 inches ginger, grated
- 1 tbsp lime juice
- 3 tbsp soy sauce

For fresh herbs:

- ½ cup finely chopped chives
- ½-1 cup chopped basil leaves
- 3 sliced spring onions
- 1 cup bean sprouts
- 1 cup chopped coriander

Preparation Time - 20 minutes

Serving Size - 2

Instructions:

1. Boil a large pot of water and cook the rice noodles in them until they are slightly soft and take off the heat.

2. Add the paste ingredients to a blender and blend till smooth. Keep aside.

3. Add oil to a preheated wok. Add the tofu with ½ of the paste and 2 tbsp of broth.

4. Stir till the tofu is warmed and fragrant. In case it dries out, add more vegetable broth.

5. Push the ingredients to a side and add some oil and the noodles. Fry the noodles in the wok for about a minute.

6. Taste the dish. Add more soy sauce or chili if needed.

7. Remove from the heat and toss with the herbs and sprouts.

8. Garnish the noodles with the peanuts and lemon wedges and serve hot.

Fast and Furious - Thai style

Good news for all rice and noodle lovers, rice is a staple in Thai cuisine and thus is found in most of the traditional dishes. Rice noodles are a very popular base for a number of Thai noodle dishes. Here is the recipe for one such noodle dish, which is easy and quick to make. The spicy taste with a subtle underlying taste of honey will enthrall your taste buds and keep you craving for more!

Ingredients:

- 16 ounces Rice Noodles
- 2 Tablespoon of vegetable oil
- 1 1/2 - 4 1/2 teaspoon of red pepper flakes to suit your spice buds
- 1/2 tablespoon of chili paste
- 1/3 - 1/2 cup toasted sesame oil
- 1/3 cup of honey
- ⅓ cup of soy sauce
- Garnish – Scallions, peanuts, carrots, cilantro, sesame seeds, and Sriracha.

Preparation Time – 20 minutes

ServingSize –6

Instructions:

1. Chop all the ingredients finely and set them aside to be used for garnishing purposes later

2. In a pot, heat water till it boils and add a teaspoon of salt. Add the rice noodles and let it cook properly.

3. Drain the rice noodles and rice with cold water to stop the cooking and set it aside.

4. Heat oil in a large saucepan and add the pepper flakes considering your likeness for spice.

5. Once the oil is hot, strain the pepper flakes and keep the oil aside.

6. In a saucepan, add the strained oil and chili paste. Whisk it thoroughly and then add the soy sauce and honey.

7. Add the rice noodles and toss till properly mixed.

8. The noodles can be served at any temperature of your convenience.

9. Do not forget to garnish before you eat!

Chicken and Shrimp Delight - Pad Thai

Pad Thai is a traditional Thai street delicacy and is made mostly of stir-fried rice noodles. It is made with a variety of meat options. Vegetarians have the option of going for tofu as their choice of protein for this noodle dish. The signature tangy sweetness of this dish comes from the Pad Thai sauce, a rich aromatic sauce that finds its roots deep in Thai culture. Though the more common sauce is made with tamarind, traditional Pad Thai was created without tamarind as you will see in this recipe below.

Ingredients:

For the Pad Thai:

- 8 ounces pad thai rice noodles
- 10 - 15 medium-sized raw shrimp with shells removed.
- 1 egg
- 1 1/2 tablespoons soy sauce
- 2 cups bean sprouts
- 3 - 4 minced garlic cloves
- 1/3 cup of dry roasted and finely chopped unsalted peanuts
- 1 teaspoon of grated ginger
- 2 - 3 tablespoons of vegetable oil
- 1 - 2 finely sliced green or red chilies
- 4 sliced green onions
- 1 lemon cut into wedges
- 1 boneless chicken breast/ 1 to 2 boneless thighs, chopped into small pieces.

For the Pad Thai Sauce

- 3 to 4 tablespoons brown sugar
- 1/3 cup of chicken stock
- 3 tablespoons rice or white vinegar
- 3 teaspoon lemon juice
- 1/4 teaspoon cayenne pepper
- 3 teaspoon soy sauce
- 3 tablespoons fish sauce

Preparation Time - 40 minutes
Serving Size - 3
Instructions:

1. Mix all the sauce ingredients in a cup and stir continuously until all the sugar dissolves.

2. Marinate the chopped chicken in soy sauce and keep aside.

3. In a large pot, boil hot water and add the rice noodles. Boil the noodles till soft but they must have some crunchiness retained. Rinse them in cold water to stop cooking.

4. Add oil, chili, ginger, and garlic to a frypan and sauté till light brown.

5. Add the chicken and stir for 2 minutes till it turns opaque.

6. Add shrimp and stir for another few minutes till the shrimp turns pinkish-orange.

7. Fry till the pan dries up a bit. Then add 1-2 tablespoons of the sauce, just enough to keep the ingredients frying.

8. Push the ingredients to one side. Crack an egg and whisk it fast to scramble it.

9. Add the noodles with 2 more tablespoons of the sauce. Carefully mix the noodles using two utensils. Keep

on adding a few tablespoons of the sauce at a time to ensure that it spreads evenly. Cook until the noodles turn soft and slightly chewy. This should take about 8-10 minutes.

10. Fold in the bean sprouts and cut off the heat

11. Add fish sauce until you get the taste you desire.

12. Garnish it with lemon wedges and chopped nuts and serve.

Flowing Ecstacy - Thai River Noodles

River Noodles, a wide flat noodle variety are a much sought after delicacy in Thailand. These noodles are best served just like Mother Nature, fresh, and aromatic. Made with a diversity of vegetable and meat combinations, every bite into this noodle dish will let you envision the beauty of nature, complete with a soft flowing texture that will leave you hungry for more.

Ingredients:

- 32 ounces of river noodles
- 2 to 3 tablespoons sherry (a type of grape wine)

- 12 - 16 ounces of cut strips of chicken breast or thigh
- 2 cups Chinese broccoli
- 1 egg
- 4 cloves of minced garlic
- 1/2 cup fresh coriander

For Marination of chicken

- 6 teaspoons of soy sauce
- 3 teaspoons of oyster sauce
- 1 teaspoon brown sugar
- For Stir-Fry Sauce
- 3 teaspoons of soy sauce
- 6 teaspoons of fish sauce
- 1 teaspoon dark soy sauce
- 3 teaspoons lime juice
- 1/3 to 1/2 teaspoon of cayenne pepper
- 1/4 teaspoon white pepper

Preparation Time - 40 minutes
Serving Size - 4
Instructions:

1. Take the chicken in a large bowl and add the mixture of all the marination ingredients. Mix thoroughly to ensure equal application of the marinade on all surfaces and set aside to marinate.

2. Add all the ingredients for the stir fry sauce in a cup and keep it close to the stove.

3. Add 2 tablespoons of oil to a frying pan kept on

medium heat. Add garlic and stir fry for a few seconds to ensure proper release of fragrance.

4. Add the chicken and keep on stir-frying it till it is cooked. If the wok becomes excessively dry, a tbsp of sherry should be added to keep the frying process continued.

5. Add vegetables and stir - fry them till they are soft but still green and add sherry in case the pan dries again.

6. Push the ingredients aside and add an egg. Whisk it quickly to scramble it.

7. Add the noodles and the stir fry sauce and gently toss the entire contents till the noodles are consistent in color and have softened.

8. Add the fish sauce and the lemon juice according to your desired taste.

9. Serve the noodles and drizzle freshly chopped coriander on the top.

Thin Lines - Pancit Bihon

There is a very thin line between tasty food and absolute ecstasy, and this dish is an exemplary example for the same. It's made from traditional Filipino rice noodles called

Bihon.The specialty of these noodles is the slick thinness of every strand and is super easy to cook. Loaded with fresh veggies and protein of your choice, it is a very delicious meal indeed. You can stick to the recipe or can also experiment with your garden. We've used chicken as our choice of protein for this dish. Quick and easy to make, this dish is ideal for any time of the day and will add a splash of freshness with every bite.

Ingredients:

- 16 ounces of sliced chicken breast (boneless)
- 8 ounces of Bihon noodles
- 1 tablespoon of peanut oil
- 1 finely chopped small onion
- 2 cloves of finely chopped garlic
- Lemon wedges
- 1 ½ cup of chopped mixed vegetables such as carrot, cabbage, green beans, broccoli, etc.
- Pepper
- Salt

For the Pancit Sauce:

- 2 cups of chicken stock
- 1 teaspoon of oyster sauce
- 2 tablespoons of soya sauce
- 2 tablespoons of dark soya sauce
- 1 teaspoon sugar

Preparation Time - 20 minutes

Serving Size - 4

Instructions:

1. Add oil and chicken to a large frypan kept over medium heat. Cook until it is soft and tender and then set aside.

2. Cook onion and garlic for 2 minutes and then add the chicken with some salt and pepper seasoning to taste.

3. Add the vegetables and cook until the vegetables become tender.

4. Mix the contents of the Pancit Sauce in a cup and stir till the sugar completely dissolves.

5. Add the Pancit Sauce and let the contents boil.

6. Add the Bihon noodles to the frypan and mix till the sauce coats all the contents evenly.

7. Cook the noodles till they become soft. Do not let them overcook.

8. You may add more stock or water if the pan dries out before the noodles are completely cooked.

9. Finish with salt and pepper seasoning. Add soy sauce if you feel the need.

10. Place the lemon wedges in the bowls with the noodles and your dish is ready to serve.

Lo Filipino!

Lo Mein is a must at parties in the Philippines! These Filipino Stir-Fried Noodles are similar to chow mein, and though it's meant for a fun, festive atmosphere, it's also a perfect dish for a romantic dinner or a heavenly dinner. It's simple to make and uses a myriad of vegetables which can be customized as per your liking. Its generally made from chicken, pork, and shrimp, but can also be made into a vegetarian dish that will take your tastebuds out for a spin. In this recipe, we have skipped the pork, but the dish will still be satiating your deepest, hungriest desires.

Ingredients:

- 1 cup of bok choy
- 1 cup of thinly sliced cabbage
- I cup of green beans, sliced
- ½ cup of celery, chopped
- 1 cup of carrots, chopped
- ½ cup of chopped cilantro
- 1 cup finely chopped onions
- 2 tablespoons of oil
- 1 tablespoon of minced garlic
- 8 ounces shrimp, shelled
- Salt and pepper to taste
- 2 tablespoons of soy sauce
- 2 cups of chicken broth
- 1 tablespoon Worcestershire sauce
- 8 ounces of Lo Mein egg noodles
- Lemon wedges or slices

Preparation Time - 45 minutes

Serving Size - 8

Instructions:

1. Boil water in a pot and cook noodles until soft. Drain and set aside.

2. Blanch vegetables in a mixture of boiling water and salt for about a minute.

3. Prepare an ice bath in a large bowl and transfer the blanched vegetables. Once the vegetables cool down, transfer them to a paper-lined plate.

4. Take a large frypan and add oil and heat over medium flame. Add onion and garlic and cook until the onion turns translucent.

5. Add the shrimp and cook until it turns slightly pink and curls up. Remove the shrimp from the frypan and set it aside.

6. Add the chicken broth, soy sauce, Worcestershire sauce, and water and let it boil. Add salt to taste. Let the contents simmer for 5 minutes.

7. Add the noodles and lightly toss them so that they absorb the sauce. If it feels too dry, you may add water. Cook until soft and then add the shrimp and vegetables.

8. Divide the noodles into serving bowls and garnish with lemon slices and cilantro. You may add lemon juice for some extra tanginess.

Seafood Palabok

Palabok is a traditional Filipino thin rice noodle dish, made primarily from seafood. The Palabok sauce is rich and creamy and contains a combination of different seafood, each with its unique taste balancing out the other. A delicacy in the Philippines, this dish will take you straight to the heart of the beautiful island country with its aromas and rich fragrances.

Ingredients:

- 18 ounces of thin Bihon noodles
- Palabok Sauce
- 6 ounces crab fat
- 6 ounces of crab meat
- 3 tbsp of annatto powder
- Fish sauce
- ½ cup of flakes of smoked fish
- 4 cloves of minced garlic
- 1 minced red onion
- 3 tbsp of cornstarch
- Oil

Palabok Toppings

- Sliced rings of squid
- Unshelled mussels
- Shrimps, unshelled
- Thinly chopped spring onions
- Sliced lemons
- Fried finely chopped garlic
- Sliced hard-boiled eggs

Preparation Time - 60 min
Serving Size - 4
Instructions:

1. Cook the Bihon noodles in boiling water until soft. Drain and keep them aside.

2. To make the sauce, add 2 cups of water to a pot and boil the squid, shrimps, and mussels. Drain the liquid and keep the seafood aside.

3. Shell the shrimps. Take the shells and grind it thoroughly. Strain the shells through a muslin cloth to extract all the juice. Pour the water used for boiling on the shell powder and drain. Keep this aside.

4. Remove the shells from the mussel and set aside.

5. Blend the crab meat, fat, boiled water, fish sauce and annatto powder in a blender.

6. Sauté garlic and onion in a pan of oil.

7. Add the fish flakes and blended mixture.

8. Take a separate container and add cornstarch mixed with water to it. Ensure that there are no lumps in the paste.

9. Boil the sauce and then simmer till it becomes thick. You may add water if the thickness increases too much. Take the sauce off the heat.

10. Take the noodles on a plate and pour the sauce over it. Garnish it with the cooked seafood, chopped spring onions, eggs, and fried garlic.

11. Squeeze the lemons over the dish to add some extra tanginess.

Asian Garlic Delight

Garlic, a supremely fragrant condiment, when incorporated well with any dish, brings out the dish in a whole new light. Having garlic as one of the highlighting ingredients thus adds up as the cherry on the cake. These Asian style garlic noodles are easy to make and a must for parties, social gatherings, or just family dinners. With a light aromatic sauce and shrimp, this noodle dish makes up for a wholesome meal and will successfully fill your tummy while leaving you in the seventh heaven of delight.

- Ingredients:

- 8 ounces of spaghetti
- 12 ounces of medium shrimp, shelled.
- 8 ounces of sliced mushrooms
- 1 tablespoon of olive oil
- 2 diced zucchinis
- 1 sliced red bell pepper
- 2 tablespoons of chopped fresh cilantro leaves
- 1 grated carrot

For the sauce:

- 1/3 cup soy sauce
- 2 tablespoons of packed brown sugar
- 3 minced garlic
- 1 tablespoon of grated ginger
- 1 tablespoon of oyster sauce
- 1 tablespoon of ground fresh chile paste, or more, to taste
- 1 teaspoon of sesame oil

Preparation Time - 30 minutes
Serving Size - 4
Instructions:

1. Mix the soy sauce, sugar, chili paste, garlic, ginger, oyster sauce, and sesame oil. Ensure the sugar completely dissolves.

2. Add salt to a pot full of boiling water and cook the spaghetti in it until soft.

3. Take olive oil in a pan and heat over medium flame.

Add the shrimp and the sauce (2tbsp) and cook until the shrimp turns pink. Remove the shrimp and set aside.

4. Add the vegetables and cook until tender. Mix in the spaghetti, shrimp and the sauce. Toss till the sauce evenly coats all the contents in the skillet.

5. Garnish with cilantro and serve!

Under-the-sea Malabon

Pancit Malabon is a dish, rich in flavor and nutrients that originated in the coastal city of Malabon, Philippines. Traditionally made from a variety of seafood such as oysters, shrimp, smoked Tinapa flakes, squid, and mussels, it's a good dish to satisfy your seafood cravings. The noodles are a different kind, thick and tough, and made from rice flour. The seafood and Filipino spice mix create a perfect balance and will add bursts of flavor in your mouth with every bite.

Ingredients:

- 16 ounces of thick rice noodles
- ¾ cups of shrimp juice

- 3 tablespoons of fish sauce
- ½ cup of annatto water (annatto seeds diluted in water)
- 1 tablespoon of minced garlic
- ½ teaspoon of salt
- 1 finely chopped onion
- 8 ounces of shelled shrimps, cooked and split into half lengthwise
- I cup of cabbage, chopped and blanched
- 4 ounces sliced adobong pusit
- Lemons, cut into quarters
- ¾ cup of Tinapa flakes
- I tablespoon of chopped parsley
- 3 sliced pieces of hard-boiled eggs
- 2 tablespoons of toasted garlic

Preparation Time - 1 hour
Serving Size - 2
Instructions:

1. Cook the noodles in boiling water until soft. Keep aside.

2. Sauté the minced onion and garlic. Add shrimp and cook the shrimp till they turn pinkish-orange.

3. Add the black pepper and fish sauce

4. Add the shrimp juice, annatto water, and boil.

5. Simmer for a few minutes (2-3 min)

6. In a bowl, place the noodles and add sauce to the mixture. Lightly toss till it is thoroughly mixed.

7. Transfer the noodles into serving bowls and garnish it with Tinapa flakes, parsley, eggs, garlic, and cabbage.

8. Serve with lemon if desired. Enjoy!

Chicken Chow Mein

Chow mein noodles are such an easy to make and an all-time favorite amongst all generations. The savory sauce is sweet and spicy and full of flavor. It complements the tender noodles beautifully. This recipe is a simplified version but is still loaded with chicken, crispy veggies, and noodles. Stir-fried in a Chinese style gravy, this dish is a must-have at home and is also a better replacement to hotel takeout!

Ingredients:

- 8 ounces of cubed chicken breast
- 10 ounces of noodles
- 1 tbsp avocado oil
- Salt and pepper
- 2 tsp of oyster sauce
- 2 chopped cloves of garlic
- 3 sliced scallions
- 2 thinly cut cabbages
- 3 tbsp oyster sauce

- 1 tbsp brown sugar
- 2 tbsp soy sauce
- ⅓ cup sherry wine

Preparation Time - 35 minutes
Serving Size - 4
Instructions:

1. Boil water in a large pot. Add salt. Pour the noodles and cook until they soften.

2. Place a frying pan over a medium flame and heat. Add the oil and oyster sauce. Then add the chicken and sprinkle salt and pepper to taste.

3. Cook the chicken without flipping on high heat for 3 minutes. Flip the chicken, lower to medium heat and cook for another 3 minutes. Remove the chicken after it is cooked.

4. Put the cabbage in the pan and cook till its wilted. Then add garlic, soy sauce, oyster sauce, sherry, and brown sugar. Simmer.

5. Add the scallions and take off the heat.

6. Add chicken, cabbage, noodles, and scallions and reheat for a few minutes. Toss lightly and serve!

Pad Thai Gai - Stir fry Chicken Noodles

Pad Thai Gai is a noodle recipe brought to you straight from the streets of Thailand. Stir-fried noodles with chicken tossed in a rich, tangy sauce are the main highlight of this dish. The garnishing made of chopped nuts and basil gives the dish a fresh and crunchy texture. There is a perfect balance of sweetness and tartness in this dish, which will definitely leave you with a smile on your face.

Ingredients:

- 8 ounces of rice noodles
- 8 ounces of chicken breast, cut into cubes
- 3 minced cloves of garlic
- ¼ cup of cabbage, grated
- ¼ cup of grated carrots
- 2 thinly sliced onions
- ⅓ cup of crushed peanuts and cashew nuts
- 1 egg
- 2 cups of bean sprouts
- 7-8 leaves of basil
- 2 tbsp vegetable oil
- ¼ cup of dry roasted peanuts, unsalted

For the stir fry sauce:

- ⅓ cup of chicken stock
- 2 tbsp of fish sauce
- 1 tbsp of soy sauce
- 3 tbsp of brown sugar
- 2 tbsp of lemon juice
- Chilli flakes

Preparation Time - 30 minutes

Serving Size - 2

Instructions:

1. Boil water in a large pot. Add salt. Pour the noodles and cook until they soften. Do not overcook them.

2. Mix the soy sauce, sugar, fish sauce, and lemon juice. Ensure the sugar completely dissolves. Use 2 tbsp to marinate the chicken.

3. Add oil to a preheated fry pan and then add garlic. Stir it for a minute.

4. Add the marinated chicken and cook for 2 minutes. Add the carrot and cabbage. If it dries up, you may add more water.

5. Push the contents aside and scramble an egg in the space.

6. Add noodles and a bit of sauce. Toss it around gently. Fry for about 30 seconds and then add more sauce. Repeat this procedure until sauce is used.

7. Add the bean sprouts and cook till tender.

8. Taste the contents. You may add fish sauce if you need more flavor.

9. Garnish with nuts, spring onions, basil leaves, and lemon wedges. Squeeze some lemon juice for that extra sourness. Enjoy!

Tropicoco

Tropical destinations are like living a dream. So, why not bring the tropics to you? With this rich coconut flavored dish, you can do just that! Aromatic, rich, and easy to prepare; these coconut noodles will bring you right to the tropics with every bite. Choose your protein source or use seafood instead! The highlight of the dish is the rich coconut broth, which gives the dish its strong flavor and fragrance. This dish is gluten-free and is thus a must-have to satiate your tropical cravings.

Ingredients:

- 8-10 ounces of rice noodles
- ⅔ cup of coconut milk
- 1 cup chicken stock
- 10-12 shelled shrimp
- 3-4 tbsp purple onion, minced
- 3 minced cloves of garlic
- 3 inches of ginger, grated
- ½ tsp chili powder
- ½ tsp finely chopped coriander

- 1 red chili, minced
- 1 bay leaf
- 1 ½ tbsp lemon juice
- 3 tbsp fish sauce
- 1 tbsp brown sugar
- 1-2 sliced spring onions
- A handful of fresh basil

Preparation Time - 25 minutes
Serving Size - 2
Instructions:

1. Boil a large pot of water and cook the rice noodles in them until they are slightly soft and take off the heat.

2. Boil chicken stock in a deep frying pan. Add the onions, ginger, garlic, coriander, chili powder, chili, and bay leaf. Let it boil for another 2 minutes.

3. Add the shrimp and reduce the heat. Let the mixture simmer until the shrimp is cooked.

4. Lower the heat further and add the fish sauce, brown sugar, lemon juice, coconut milk and stir well. Ensure that the sugar completely dissolves.

5. Add the noodles to the frying pan and gently toss till the sauce is properly incorporated. Remove from the heat.

6. Taste the noodles and add more fish sauce or lemon juice if you feel the need. If it is too spicy, you may add coconut milk.

7. Garnish with the spring onions and basil and drizzle some coconut milk and serve!

A Spice of Life

This noodle recipe is an adaptation of the traditional Kao Soy from Thailand. The highlight of this dish is the burst of flavors, courtesy of the spice mix in this dish. A number of different condiments mingle together to give a perfect balance and provide a sense of delightful comfort. Made from egg noodles, this dish will certainly take your taste buds out for the ride of their life.

Ingredients:

- 2 to 4 bundles of egg noodles
- 1/2 packet of tofu, cubed
- 1 red bell pepper
- ½ cup chopped coriander
- 1 green bell pepper
- 1 handful mushrooms
- 3-4 lemon wedges
- 2 sliced spring onions
- 1/2 cup of coconut milk
- 2 tablespoons of oil
- 3 tablespoons of soy sauce
- 8 ounces shrimp, peeled and deveined

For the curry paste:

- 1 to 2 chilis
- 1/2 teaspoon turmeric
- 3 garlic cloves, minced
- 3 inches ginger, grated
- 1 teaspoon of cumin
- 3 teaspoon finely chopped coriander
- 1/4 teaspoon ground cloves
- 1/4 teaspoon ground cinnamon
- 1/2 teaspoon ground cardamom
- 2 tablespoons fish sauce
- Sugar

Preparation Time - 30 minutes
Serving Time - 2
Instructions:
1. Boil water in a large pot. Add salt. Pour the egg noodles and cook until they soften. Do not overcook them.

2. For the curry paste, add all the ingredients in a blender and blend thoroughly until smooth.

3. Add oil to a heated wok and add the paste. Stir to unleash the fragrance.

4. Mix some tbsp of coconut milk and vegetable and stir nicely until the mushrooms are cooked and bell peppers turn bright. You may add more coconut milk if the wok dries out.

5. Add all the coconut milk along with the soy sauce, noodles, shrimp and stir fry together.

6. Toss the noodles lightly to ensure proper mixing of the ingredients till the noodles soak most of the curry sauce.

7. Serve them fresh and hot, straight from the wok, with a garnishing of coriander and green onion. Add lime juice for the extra tanginess.

Bun Ga Nuong - Lemongrass Chicken

These Vietnamese style noodles satisfy your cravings for a refreshing, nutritious, and rich flavor-packed meal. Most commonly made with rice vermicelli, the added crunch of the fresh veggies, tangy sauce, and juicy, tender lemongrass chicken will cause your mouth to water just by thinking about it. The garnish made of crushed peanuts and cilantro will give the dish a wonderfully fresh and nutty texture, which will feel good in your mouth. This dish is light and comforting yet fills the stomach and will satisfy your food cravings until you feel euphoric.

Ingredients:

- 20 ounces chicken
- 12 ounces of rice vermicelli
- 2 cups of chopped red cabbage
- 2 cups of bean sprouts
- 2 julienne cucumbers

- 1 julienned bell pepper
- 1 cup of snow peas
- 2 tbsp chopped cilantro
- Crushed peanuts
- 1 cup of julienned carrots

Marinade:

- 3 tbsp of Lemongrass stalks
- ¼ cup minced shallots
- 1 tbsp sweet chili sauce
- 1 tbsp Thai red curry paste
- 1 tbsp olive oil
- 3 minced cloves of garlic
- 2 tsp grated ginger
- 1 tsp dried basil
- 3 tbsp soy sauce
- 3 tbsp fish sauce
- 2 tbsp lemon juice
- 2 tbsp brown sugar

Dressing:

- 3 tbsp Reserve marinade
- 2 tbsp rice vinegar
- ¼ cup of coconut milk
- 2 tbsp fish sauce
- 2 tbsp honey
- 2 tbsp lime juice

Garnish:

- Chopped cilantro
- Lemon juice
- Crushed peanuts
- Cilantro

Preparation Time - 45 minutes
Serving Size - 4
Instructions:
Lemongrass Chicken Marinade:
In a large bowl, mix all of the marinade ingredients. Set aside 3 tbsp of this marinade for later use. Add chicken to the marinade and coat evenly. Marinate 30 minutes in the refrigerator. Bring back to room temperature for 30 minutes.

Noodle Bowl:
1. Mix all the dressing ingredients and 3 tbsp of the marinade in a small bowl.

2. Place the chicken in a pan of hot oil. Cook until its beautifully brown on one side and flip and repeat for the other side. Let the chicken cool for 5 minutes before slicing it. This ensures a juicier chicken.

3. To the same skillet, add water for the noodles and boil. Remove from the heat and soak the noodles in this boiling water. Drain them once cooked to avoid sticking to each other.

4. Add the noodles to a large bowl and pour ¼ cup of dressing and toss gently.

5. Divide the noodles into 4 serving bowls. Strain the

dressing to remove the lemongrass pieces. Drizzle the bowl with the garnish, vegetables and the amount of desired dressing. Place the chicken slices on top and serve!

Chilli Vermicelli

Spice up your usual rice noodles and vegetable combination with a dash of chili and garlic. Add the beautiful aroma of lemongrass to the mix, and you've got yourself a first-class dish. A light, nutritious noodle recipe, this comes straight from the heart of Vietnam and will give you a good, healthy substitute for any meal of the day.

Ingredients:

- 1 lemongrass stalk, finely chopped
- 2 crushed garlic cloves
- 2 tbsp soy sauce
- 1 lemon, juiced and zested.
- 1 lemon cut into wedges
- 1 red chili, halved and chopped
- 8 ounces baby corn
- 2 tbsp sesame oil

- 24 ounces of rice vermicelli
- 1 ounce chopped coriander
- 16 ounces mixed peppers, sliced
- 2 ounces roasted peanuts, chopped

Preparation Time - 20 minutes

Serving Size - 4

Instructions:

1. Crush the chili, lemongrass, and garlic till it is a fine soft paste. Add soy sauce, half the sesame oil, and lemon juice.

2. Add the sesame oil to a large heated wok and cook baby corn and peppers until they appear to be lightly charred.

3. Soak the rice vermicelli in boiled water until soft.

4. Toss the noodles, coriander and paste together. Cook for a minute and divide into 4 bowls. Garnish with peanuts and coriander and with a side of lemon wedges, your chili vermicelli is ready to serve.

Myanmar Chicken Noodles

This Burmese dish is a must-have to add to your arsenal of recipes. Choose your favorite protein and have it served over a base of rice noodles and rich tomato gravy. These noodles are fragrant and strongly flavored and can be served either as a soup or a salad, depending on your preference. Breakfast, lunch, or even a romantic dinner date, dive into it at the time of your choosing. Indulge yourself by making this easy whenever you want and enjoy the vibrant flavors.

Ingredients:

- 16 ounces chicken, chopped
- 10 ounces of rice noodles
- 6 cloves garlic, chopped
- 2 onions, chopped
- 8 tomatoes, chopped
- 1-inch ginger, grated
- 3 tablespoons soy sauce
- 1 tablespoon tomato paste
- 2 tablespoons chili powder
- 2 scallions, chopped (to garnish)
- 2 tablespoons sugar
- 8 tablespoons peanuts, crushed
- 6 tablespoons vegetable oil

Preparation Time - 40 minutes
Serving Size - 4
Instructions:
1. Boil water in a utensil. Add the rice noodles and cook them. Once properly cooked, drain them under cold water.
2. Fry the ginger, garlic, and onion in a large wok

containing oil till golden brown.

3. Add chili powder and fry

4. Add the chicken, tomatoes, paste and stir to mix well.

5. Add sugar and soy sauce till all the sugar dissolves and the tomatoes are nicely crushed.

6. Divide the noodles into bowls and add the chicken curry, peanuts and soy sauce. The dish is now ready to serve!

Indonesian Mie Goreng

This Indonesian dish is sure to please everyone in the family. It contains perfectly cooked egg noodles, crunchy, juicy veggies, and choice of proteins, all having a wonderful sweet-tangy sauce drizzled all over it. The sauce is more towards the sweet side with an underlying subtle salty taste and the heart of the dish. An easy dish to make, it will definitely bring a smile on your face with a burst of flavor.

Ingredients:
The sauce:

- 1 tbsp+1 tsp sweet soy sauce
- 1 ½ tbsp soy sauce

- 1 tbsp oyster sauce
- 1 tbsp chili garlic paste
- ½ tbsp sesame oil

The rest:

- 16 ounces cooked egg noodles
- 5 chopped cloves of garlic
- 1 shallot, chopped
- 15-18 shrimp
- Thai chilies
- 1 cup julienned carrots
- 2 eggs
- 2 cups broccoli
- Chopped green onions
- 2 tomatoes cut into wedges

Preparation Time - 30 minutes
Serving Time - 3
Instructions:

1. Combine all the ingredients for the sauce and stir them thoroughly to dissolve all clumps.

2. Heat some oil in a wok and cook the shrimp. Set the cooked protein aside.

3. Add some more oil to the wok and add garlic, chilies, and shallots. Sauté until the shallots turn translucent.

4. Add all the vegetables (except tomatoes) and cook them with the sauce until wilted.

5. Keep the vegetables to one side and add little oil and eggs. Whisk the eggs to scramble them.

6. Add the noodles, shrimp and remaining sauce and gently toss until all sauce is well absorbed.

7. Take off the heat and add tomatoes and spring onions. Toss to mix and warm up the tomatoes.

8. Serve hot!

3

DESSERTS

Cinnamon Snow

D o you really love noodles but not a fan of spices? Do you have a sweet tooth that needs to be satiated? This recipe is just for you. Enjoy the explosion of cinnamon in your mouth with this very unique cold noodle dessert. This recipe filled with crunchy toppings and soft frosting will definitely leave your taste buds craving for more with every bite.

Ingredients:

- 8 ounces egg lo mein noodles
- sliced toasted almonds for garnish
- 1 medium-size apple
- Cinnamon Dressing
- 1 tbsp ground cinnamon
- 1/2 stick butter

- 1/4 cup brown sugar

Frosting

- 2 ounces block cream cheese
- 1/4 cup milk
- 1 tsp vanilla extract
- 1/4 cup confectioners' sugar

Preparation Time - 30 minutes
Serving Time - 4
Instructions:

1. Cook the noodles in boiling water and once cooked, immediately submerge them in cold water

2. Once they are cold enough to touch, drain the water and cover it with plastic wrap and refrigerate.

3. For the dressing, melt the butter in a pan on low heat.

4. Mix the cinnamon and sugar. Stir to remove any lumps and set aside.

5. Start on the frosting. Beat milk, vanilla, and cream cheese together until a smooth batter is formed. Transfer this to a piping bag.

6. Peel and cut the apple into thin strips.

7. Combine the noodles, apples, and dressing. Toss very gently.

8. Divide the noodles and lightly drizzle the frosting on top. You may add powdered cinnamon for a stronger taste. Top with almond slices.

Hey Honey!

A sensational dessert is traditionally Chinese, but famous throughout Asia. Noodles are soaked in a soft buttery sauce filled with the sweet taste of honey. The crunchiness of the noodles, garnished with almonds and walnut is beautifully complemented by the softness of the vanilla ice cream filling your mouth with a burst of ecstasy with every bite.

Ingredients:

- 1 ½ cup of boiled Hakka noodles
- 2-3 tbsp cornflour
- Oils
- 10-12 walnuts
- 15 almonds
- 2 tbsp butter
- 3 tbsp water
- 5 tbsp sugar
- 4 tbsp honey
- ½ tsp white sesame seeds
- ½ tsp black sesame seeds
- Vanilla ice cream

Preparation Time - 35 minutes

Serving Time - 4

Instructions:

1. Dry the boiled noodles and add cornflour to absorb any leftover moisture.

2. Deep fry the noodles in oil until crispy golden.

3. Slightly crush the noodles on absorbent paper to remove excess oil

4. Submerge the almonds in water and remove all skin.

5. Dry roast the walnuts and almonds till they get golden spots.

6. For the sauce, melt butter in a pan and add sugar and water.

7. Let the sugar caramelize.

8. Add honey and mix well on a low flame.

9. Add the sesame seeds, walnuts, and almonds. Keep some sesame seeds aside for garnishing.

10. Add the fried noodles and stir gently.

11. Switch off the flame and place the noodles on a serving plate.

12. Serve it hot with scoops of vanilla ice cream and a garnish of honey and sesame seeds.

CONCLUSION

So, what are you waiting for?

You have your collection of recipes, and now, it's time to go to the kitchen and run your show. Make that feast you've always been waiting for. Get your family or partner involved and turn this into a fun-filled experience.

Bon Appetit!

www.ingramcontent.com/pod-product-compliance
Ingram Content Group UK Ltd.
Pitfield, Milton Keynes, MK11 3LW, UK
UKHW021334150825
7422UKWH00030B/553

9 781801 491051